Published by Golden Valley Press
PO BOX 955 Enterprise, UT 84725
www.josephstevenson.com

ISBN:

978-1-947215-41-2

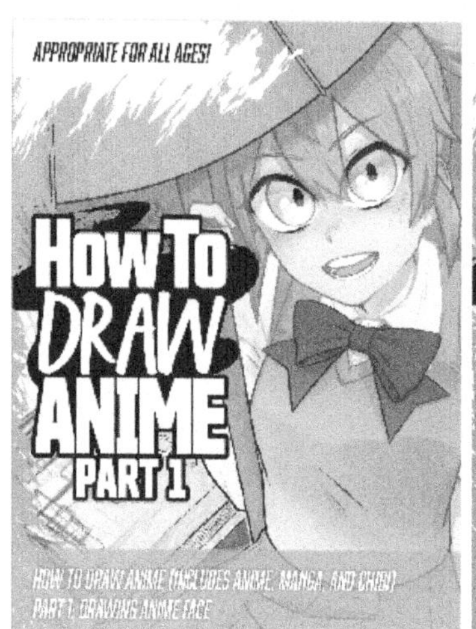
APPROPRIATE FOR ALL AGES!
HOW TO DRAW ANIME
PART 1
HOW TO DRAW ANIME (INCLUDES ANIME, MANGA, AND CHIBI)
PART 1: DRAWING ANIME FACE

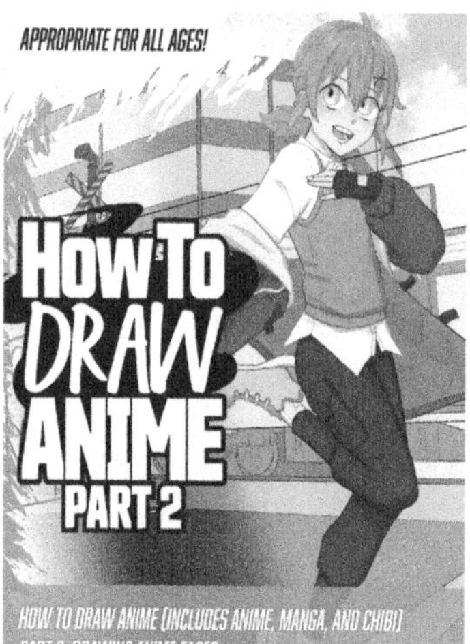
APPROPRIATE FOR ALL AGES!
HOW TO DRAW ANIME
PART 2
HOW TO DRAW ANIME (INCLUDES ANIME, MANGA, AND CHIBI)
PART 2: DRAWING ANIME FACES

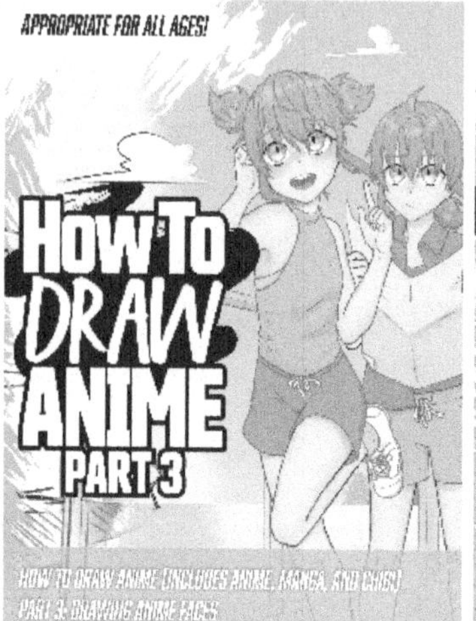
APPROPRIATE FOR ALL AGES!
HOW TO DRAW ANIME
PART 3
HOW TO DRAW ANIME (INCLUDES ANIME, MANGA, AND CHIBI)
PART 3: DRAWING ANIME FACES

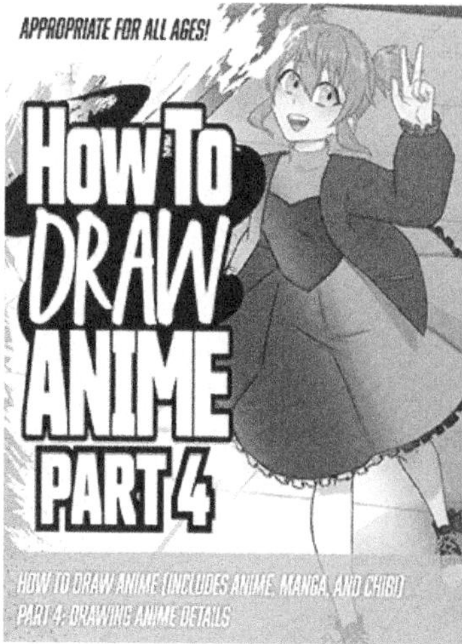
APPROPRIATE FOR ALL AGES!
HOW TO DRAW ANIME
PART 4
HOW TO DRAW ANIME (INCLUDES ANIME, MANGA, AND CHIBI)
PART 4: DRAWING ANIME DETAILS

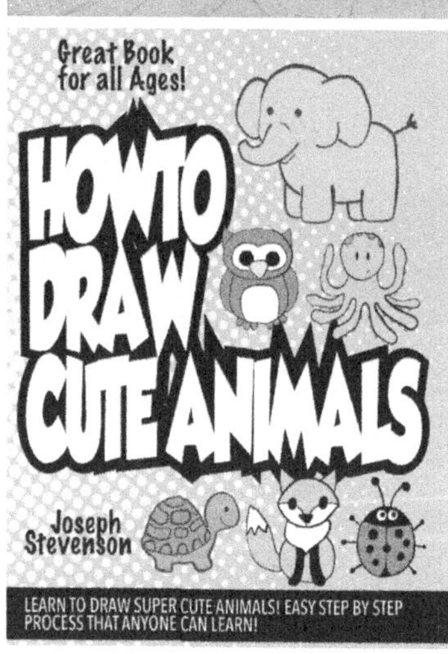
Great Book for all Ages!
HOW TO DRAW CUTE ANIMALS
Joseph Stevenson
LEARN TO DRAW SUPER CUTE ANIMALS! EASY STEP BY STEP PROCESS THAT ANYONE CAN LEARN!

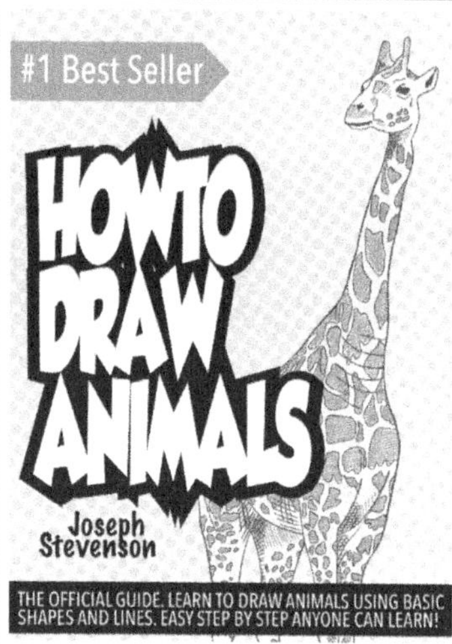
#1 Best Seller
HOW TO DRAW ANIMALS
Joseph Stevenson
THE OFFICIAL GUIDE. LEARN TO DRAW ANIMALS USING BASIC SHAPES AND LINES. EASY STEP BY STEP ANYONE CAN LEARN!

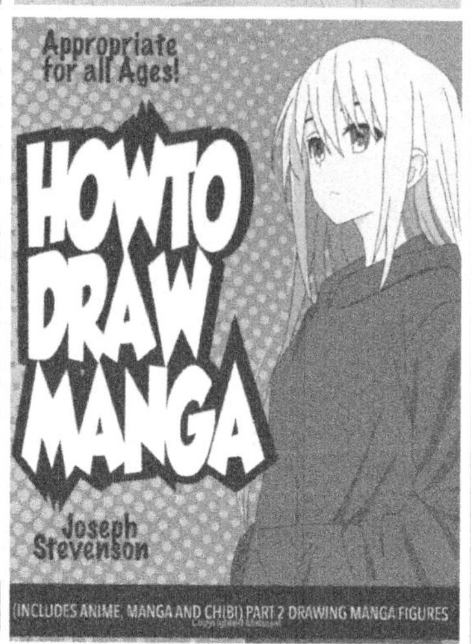
Appropriate for all Ages!
HOW TO DRAW MANGA
Joseph Stevenson
(INCLUDES ANIME, MANGA AND CHIBI) PART 2 DRAWING MANGA FIGURES

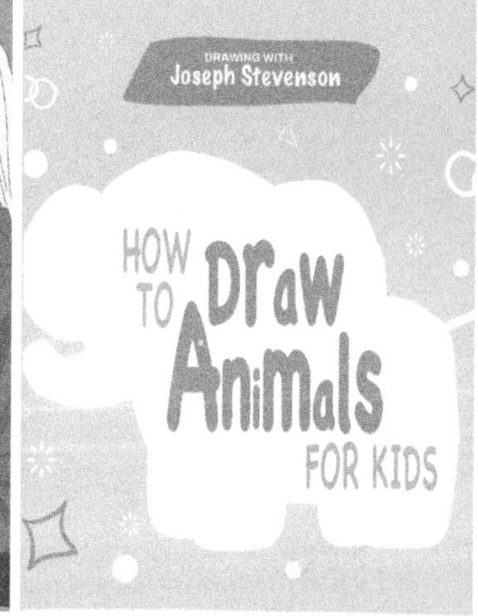
DRAWING WITH
Joseph Stevenson
HOW TO Draw Animals
FOR KIDS

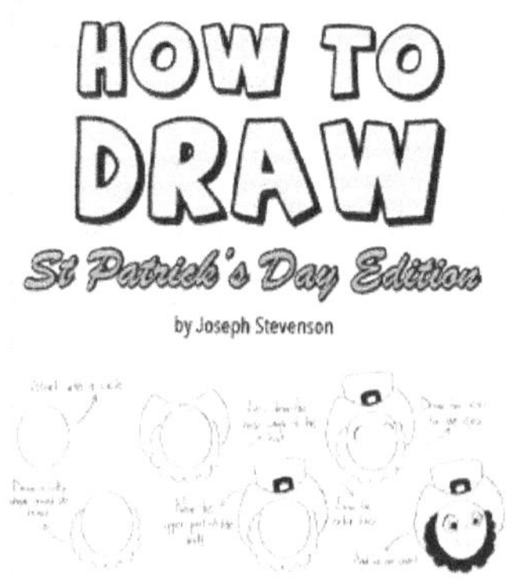
HOW TO DRAW
St Patrick's Day Edition
by Joseph Stevenson

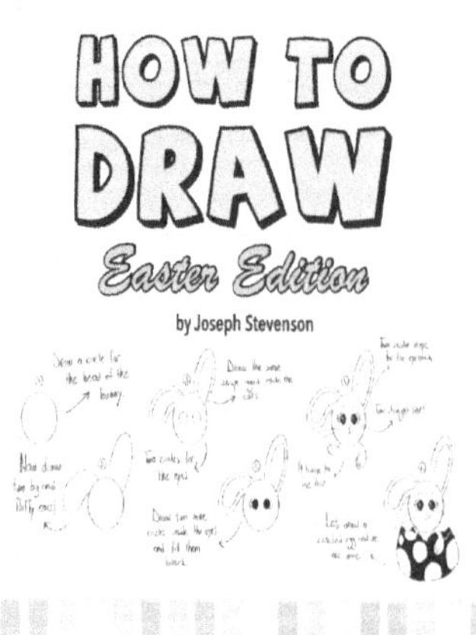
HOW TO DRAW
Easter Edition
by Joseph Stevenson

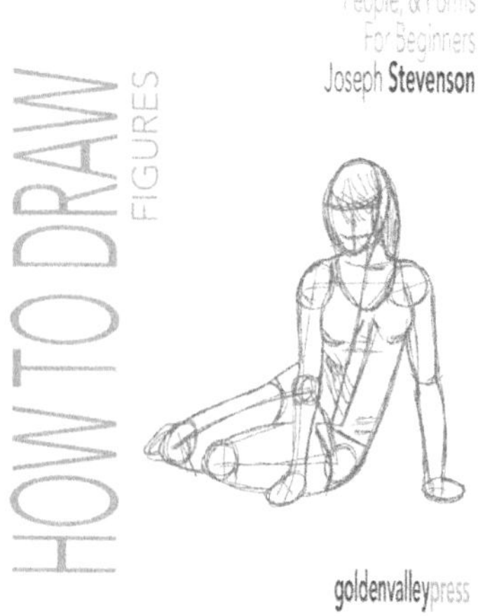
Simple Anatomy, People, & Forms For Beginners
Joseph Stevenson
HOW TO DRAW
FIGURES
goldenvalleypress

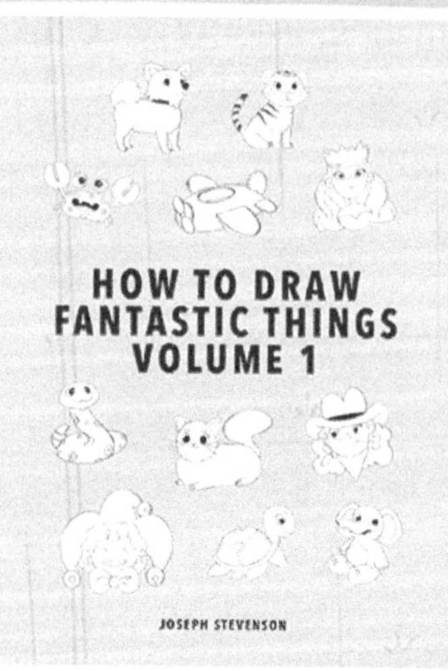
HOW TO DRAW FANTASTIC THINGS VOLUME 1
JOSEPH STEVENSON

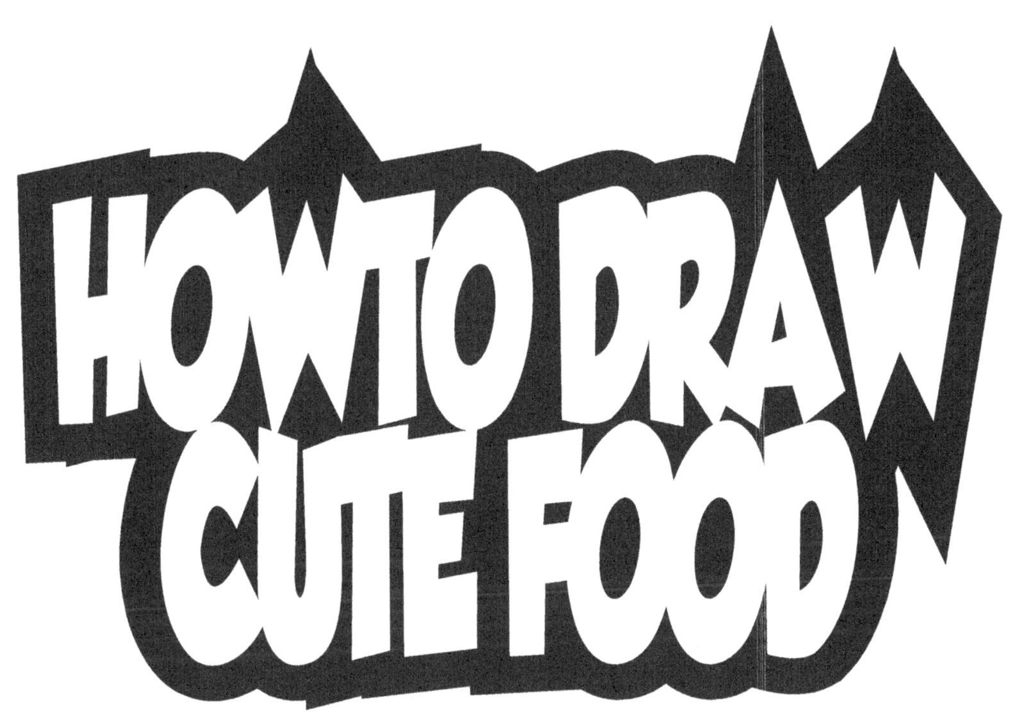
HOW TO DRAW
CUTE FOOD

INTRO

Drawing should be fun! In this book I have created a whole bunch of cute food for you to draw. You don't have to draw them just like the pictures, but instead you should draw them how you like.

When I was a kid I started out drawing cute animals on the walls of my bedroom as well as my sister's room. I did it to have fun and it helped me learn to love drawing more than I thought I ever could.

This is the second book in my how to draw cute series. The first book "how to draw cute animals" has a whole bunch of lessons on cute animals. This book focuses on cute versions of food that you can draw.

I started making these how to draw books because I wanted to help kids learn to love drawing just as much as I do. If you have any questions you can always reach out to me on my website at:

www.josephstevenson.com

In this book each lesson is on it's own page along with a section for drawing the animal yourself. I would love to see what you come up with! Please send me your own drawings on my website and I'll post them in my blog and on social media!

~ Joseph Stevenson

PIZZA

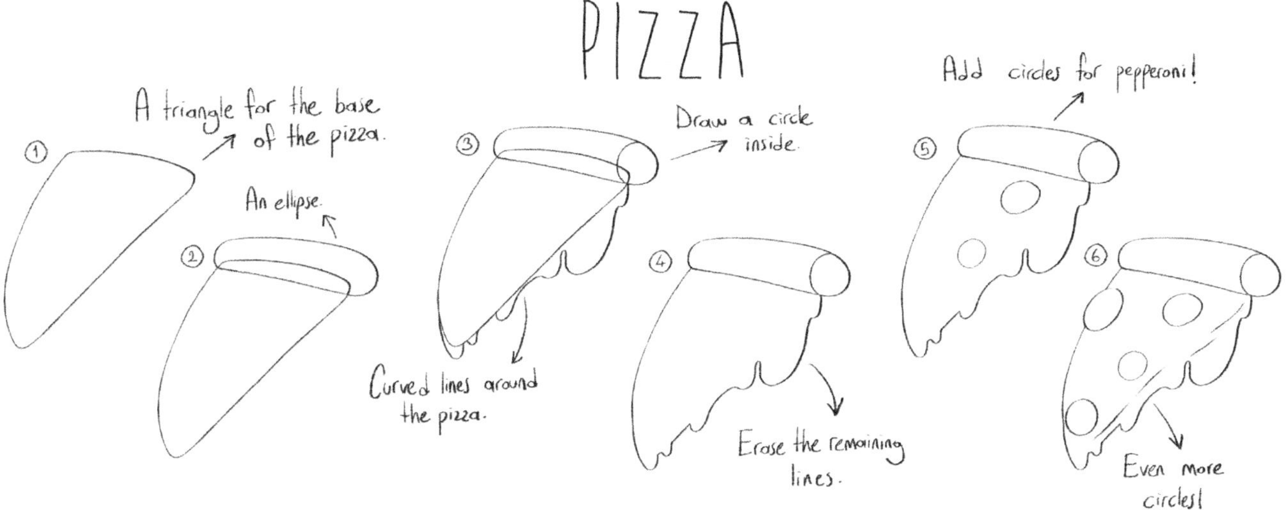

1
A triangle for the base of the pizza.
2
An ellipse.
3
Draw a circle inside.
Curved lines around the pizza.
4
Erase the remaining lines.
5
Add circles for pepperoni!
6
Even more circles!

Your turn to draw some cute food!

TACOS

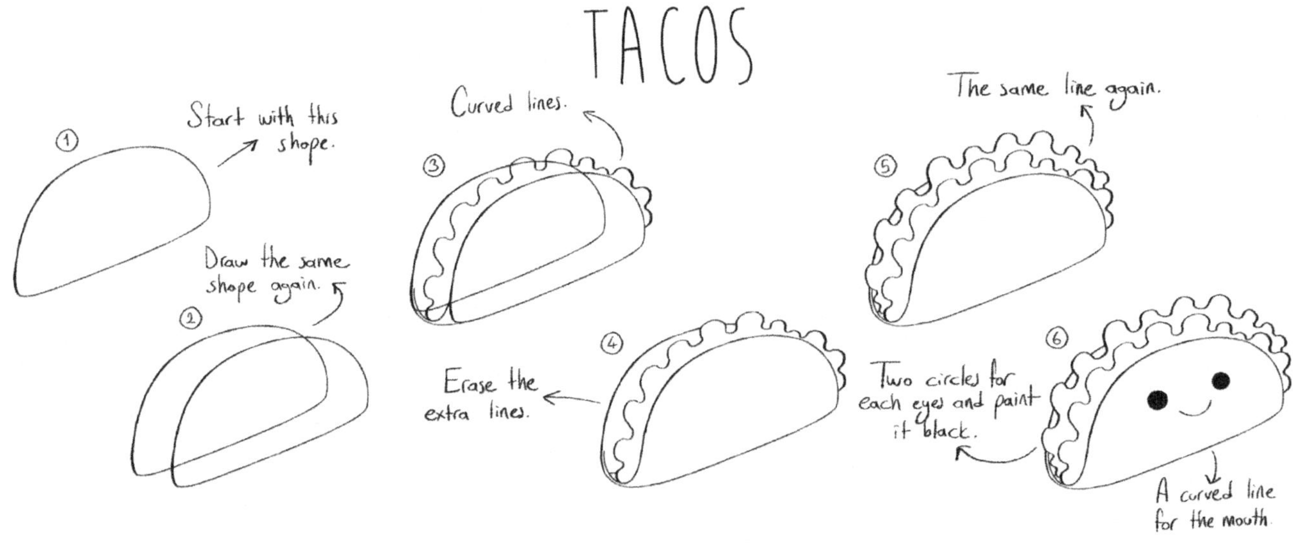

1
Start with this shape.
2
Draw the same shape again.
Curved lines.
3
Erase the extra lines.
4
The same line again.
5
Two circles for each eyes and paint it black.
6
A curved line for the mouth.

Your turn to draw some cute food!

RAMEN

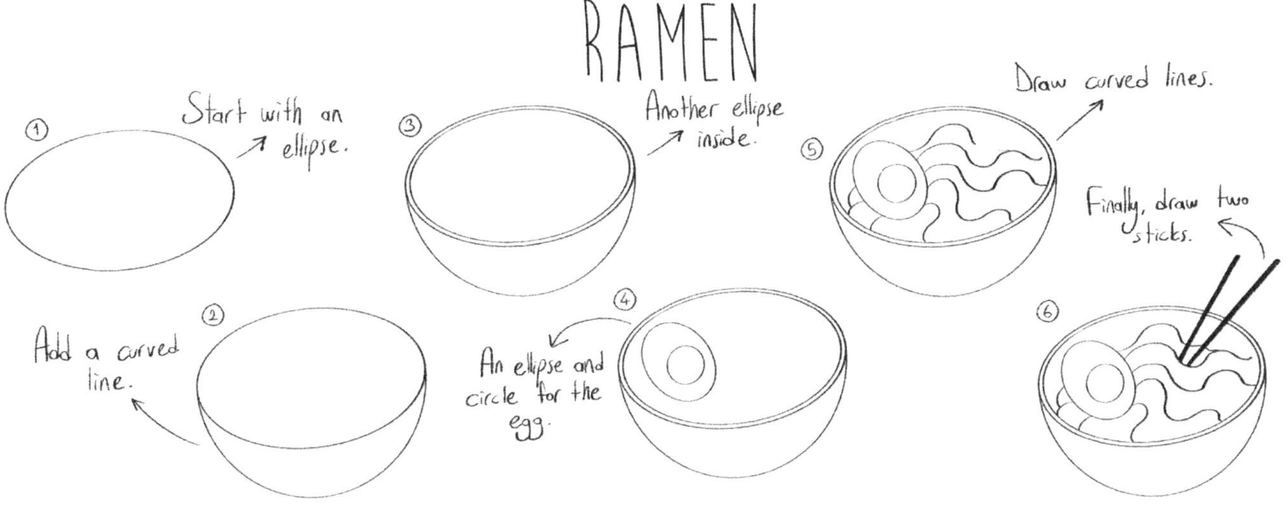

1
Start with an ellipse.
2
Add a curved line.
3
Another ellipse inside.
4
An ellipse and circle for the egg.
5
Draw curved lines.
6
Finally, draw two sticks.

Your turn to draw some cute food!

ICE CREAM

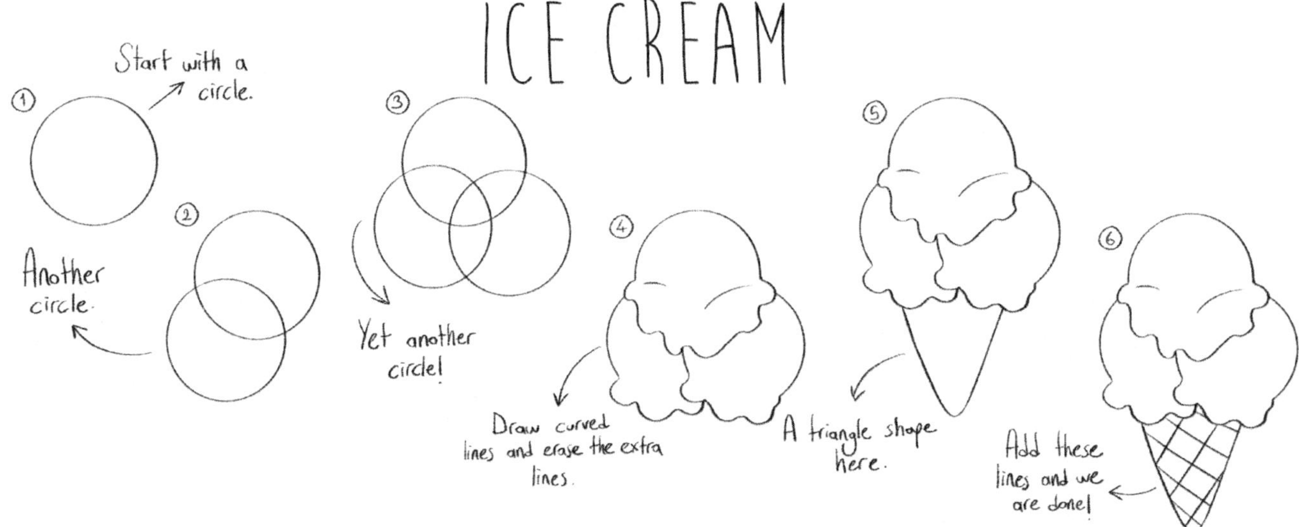

1
Start with a circle.
2
Another circle.
3
Yet another circle!
4
Draw curved lines and erase the extra lines.
5
A triangle shape here.
6
Add these lines and we are done!

Your turn to draw some cute food!

CHEESECAKE
Start with a triangle.
1
2
Two lines here.
3
Connect those two lines.
Add a black rectangle and fill it black.
4
Draw a circle.
5
Draw a fluffy shape.
A single line.
6
Curved lines.

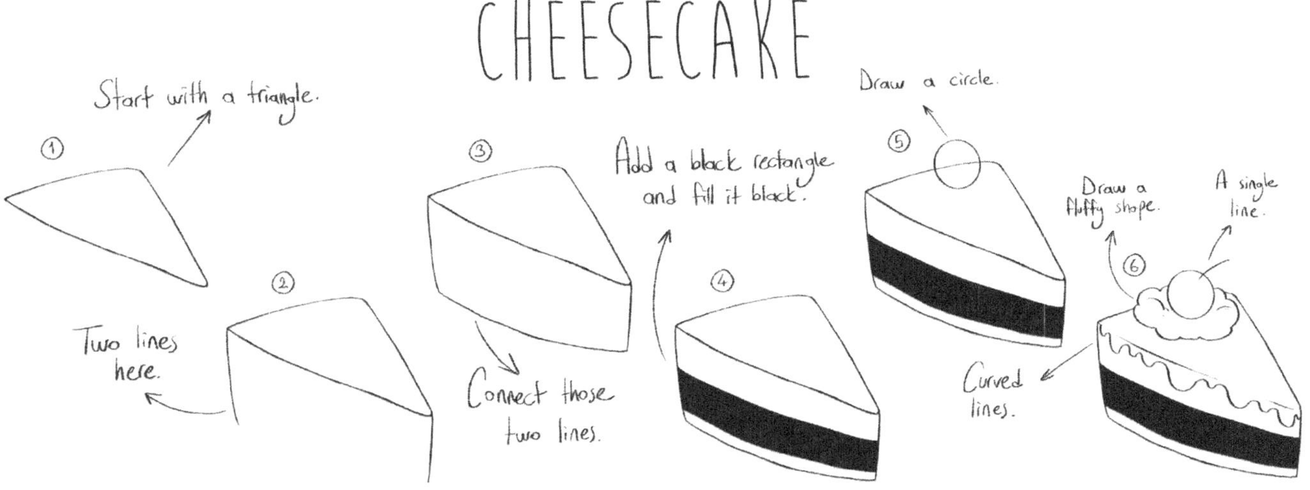

Your turn to draw some cute food!

MACARON

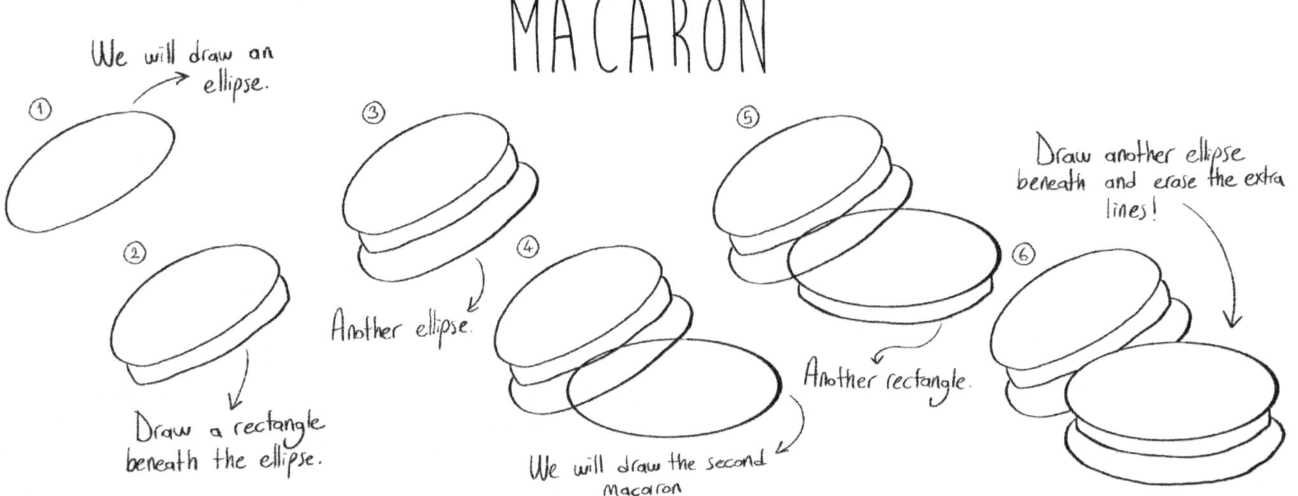

We will draw an ellipse.
1
2
Draw a rectangle beneath the ellipse.
3
Another ellipse.
4
We will draw the second macaron
5
Another rectangle.
Draw another ellipse beneath and erase the extra lines!
6

Your turn to draw some cute food!

COOKIE

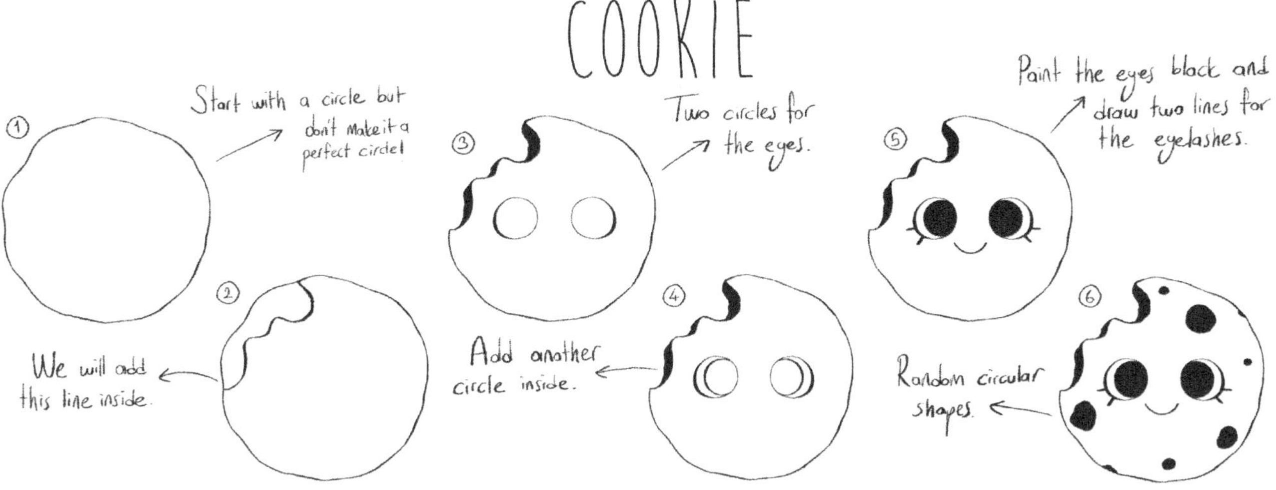

1
Start with a circle but don't make it a perfect circle!
2
We will add this line inside.
3
Two circles for the eyes.
4
Add another circle inside.
5
Paint the eyes black and draw two lines for the eyelashes.
6
Random circular shapes.

Your turn to draw some cute food!

CHURROS

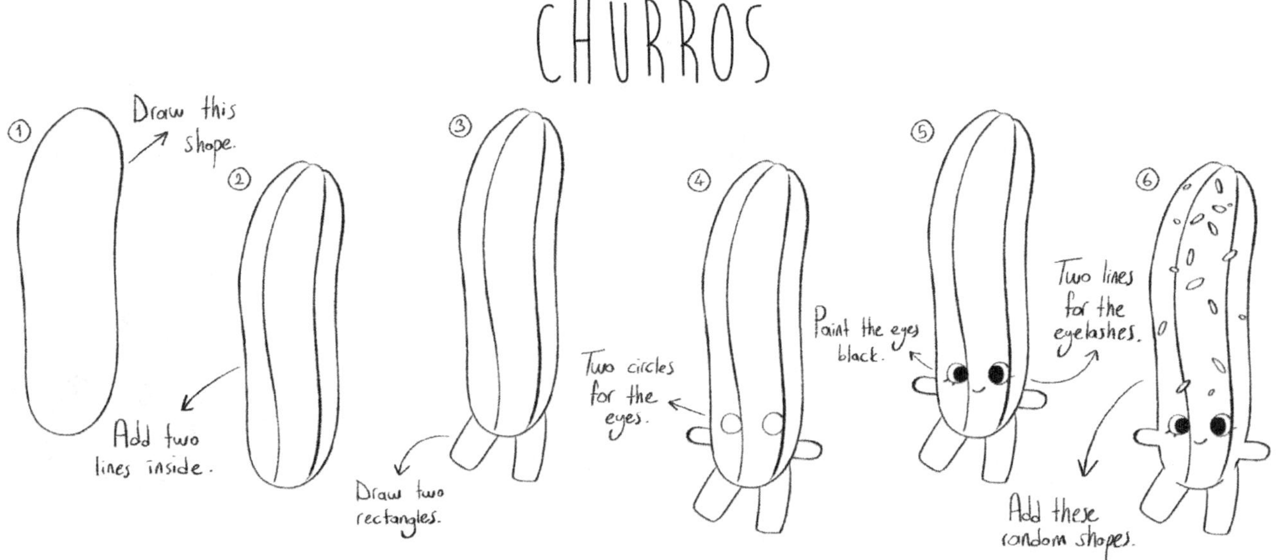

1
Draw this shape.
2
Add two lines inside.
3
Draw two rectangles.
4
Two circles for the eyes.
5
Paint the eyes black.
Two lines for the eyelashes.
6
Add these random shapes.

Your turn to draw some cute food!

MILKSHAKE
1
Think this shape as a rounded triangle.
2
Add an ellipse.
3
Lets add this line.
Connect those two shapes.
4
Draw this shape on top.
5
Add a circle.
6
Draw a line

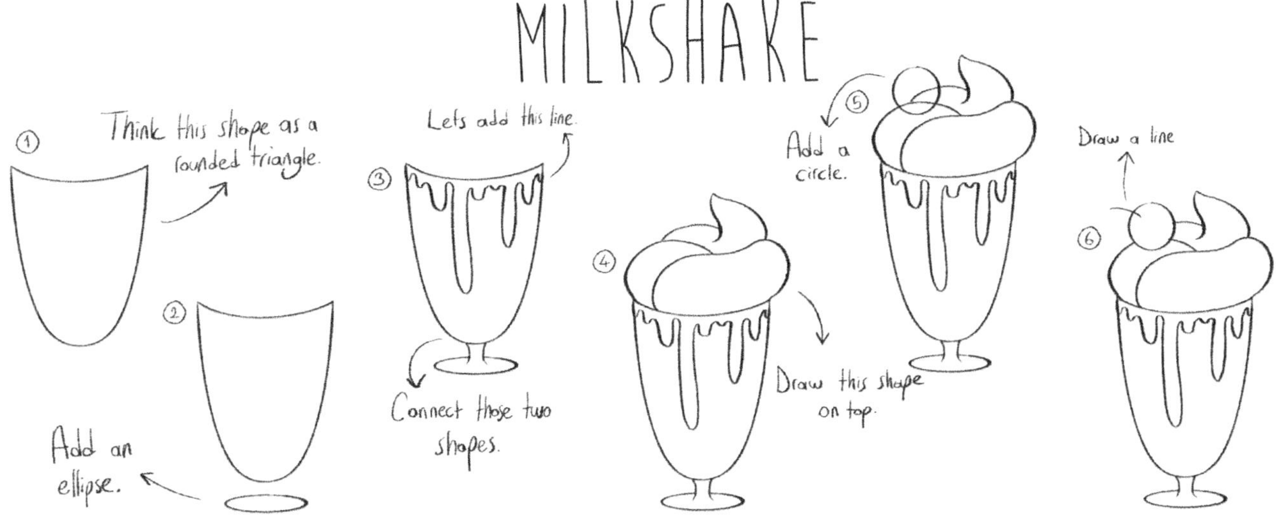

Your turn to draw some cute food!

PASTA

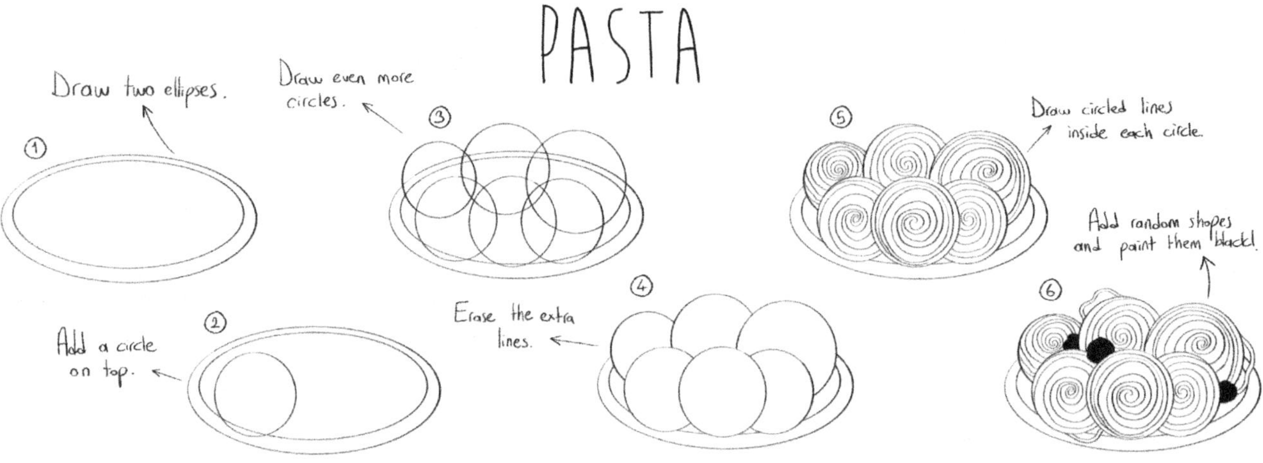

Draw two ellipses.
1
Draw even more circles.
3
5
Draw circled lines inside each circle.
Add random shapes and paint them black!
2
Add a circle on top.
4
Erase the extra lines.
6

Your turn to draw some cute food!

FRENCH FRIES

Draw a square.
1
Draw a curved line inside.
2
Add rectangles for the fries.
3
Draw more rectangles.
4
Even more rectangles!
5
6
Draw a cute face and we are done!

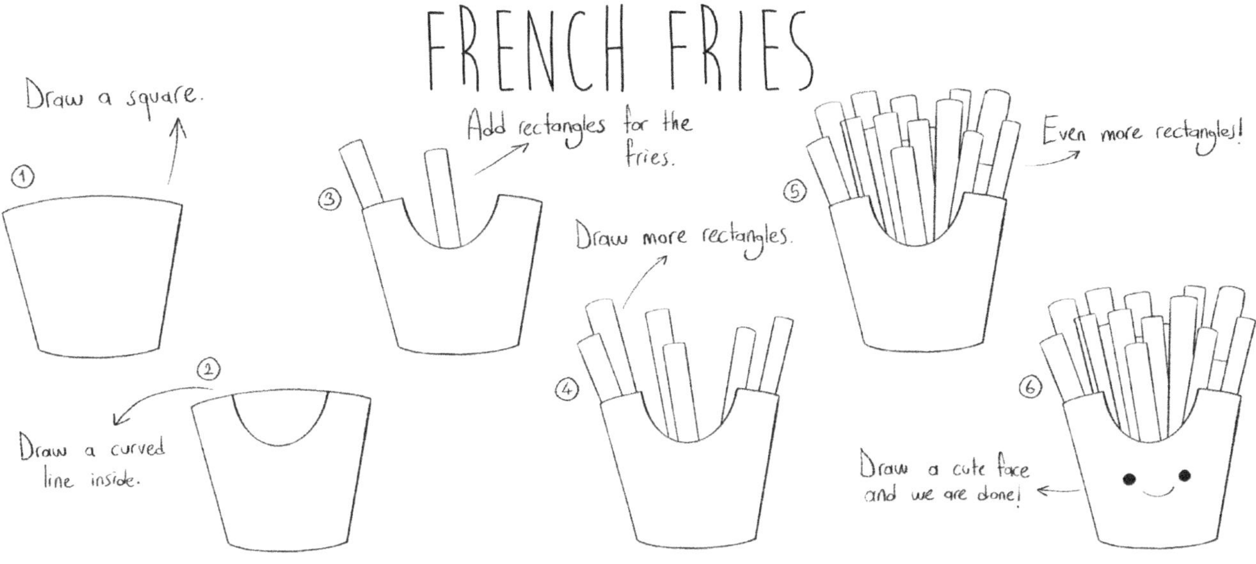

Your turn to draw some cute food!

DUMPLING

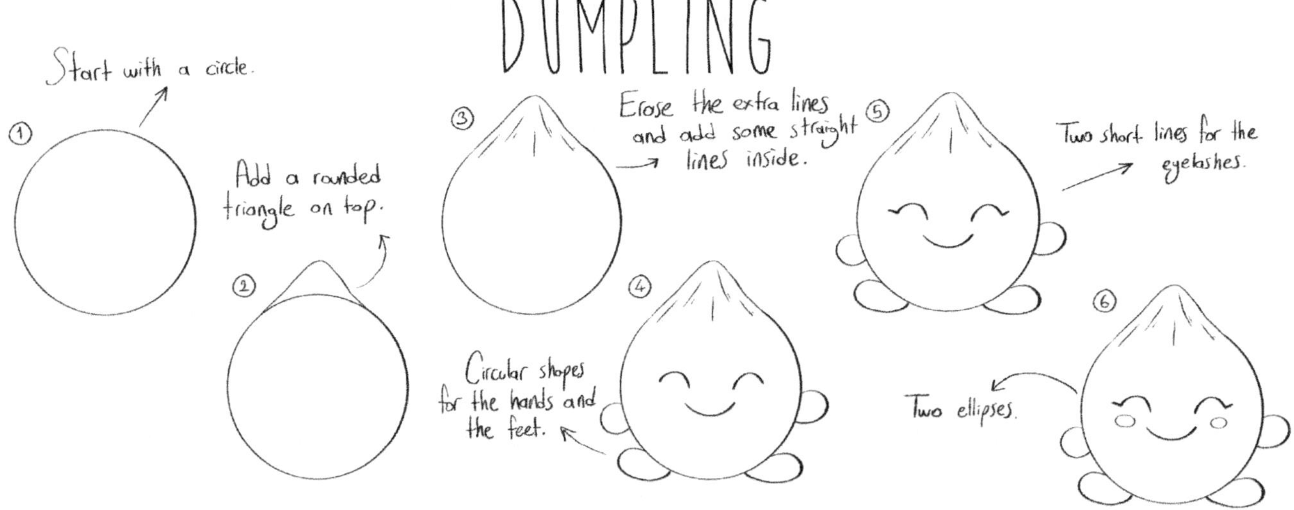
Start with a circle.
1
Add a rounded triangle on top.
2
3
Erase the extra lines and add some straight lines inside.
4
Circular shapes for the hands and the feet.
5
Two short lines for the eyelashes.
6
Two ellipses.

Your turn to draw some cute food!

HAMBURGER

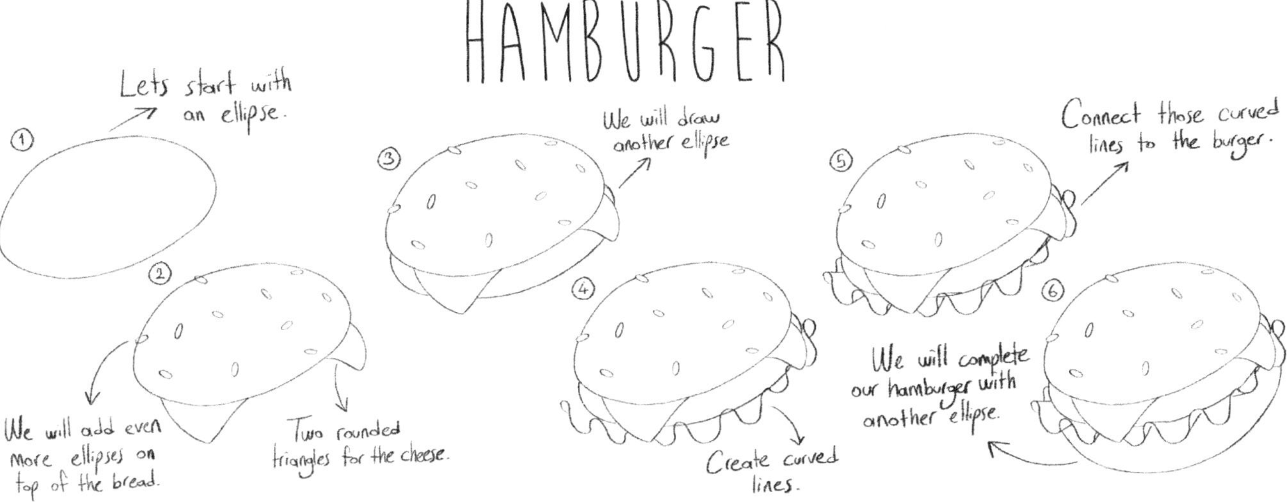
1
Lets start with an ellipse.
2
We will add even more ellipses on top of the bread.
Two rounded triangles for the cheese.
3
We will draw another ellipse
4
Create curved lines.
5
Connect those curved lines to the burger.
6
We will complete our hamburger with another ellipse.

Your turn to draw some cute food!

HOT DOG

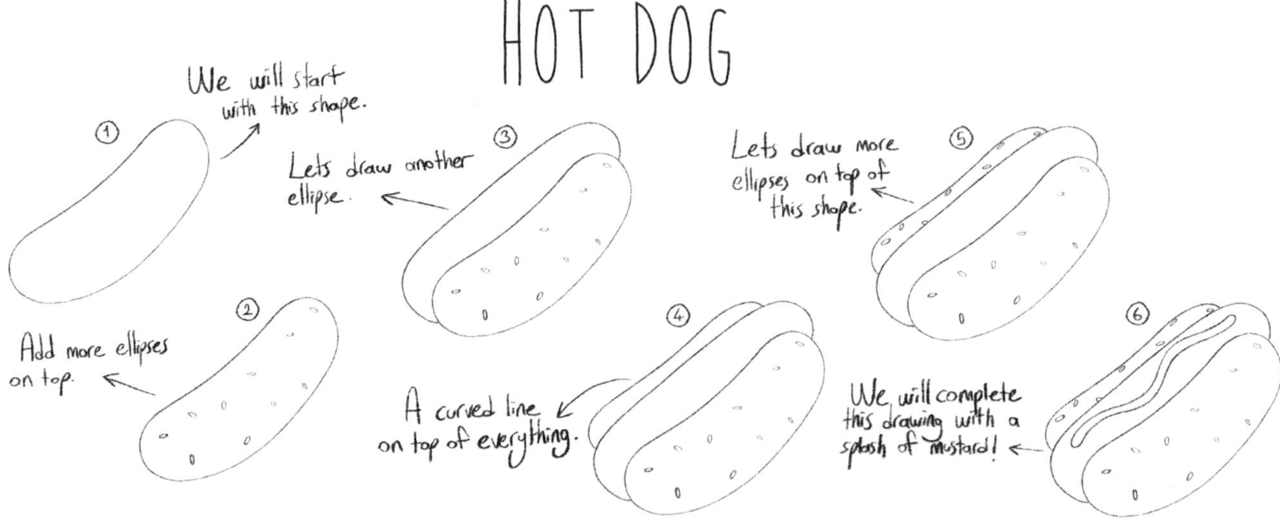

1
We will start with this shape.
2
Add more ellipses on top.
3
Lets draw another ellipse.
4
A curved line on top of everything.
5
Lets draw more ellipses on top of this shape.
6
We will complete this drawing with a splash of mustard!

Your turn to draw some cute food!

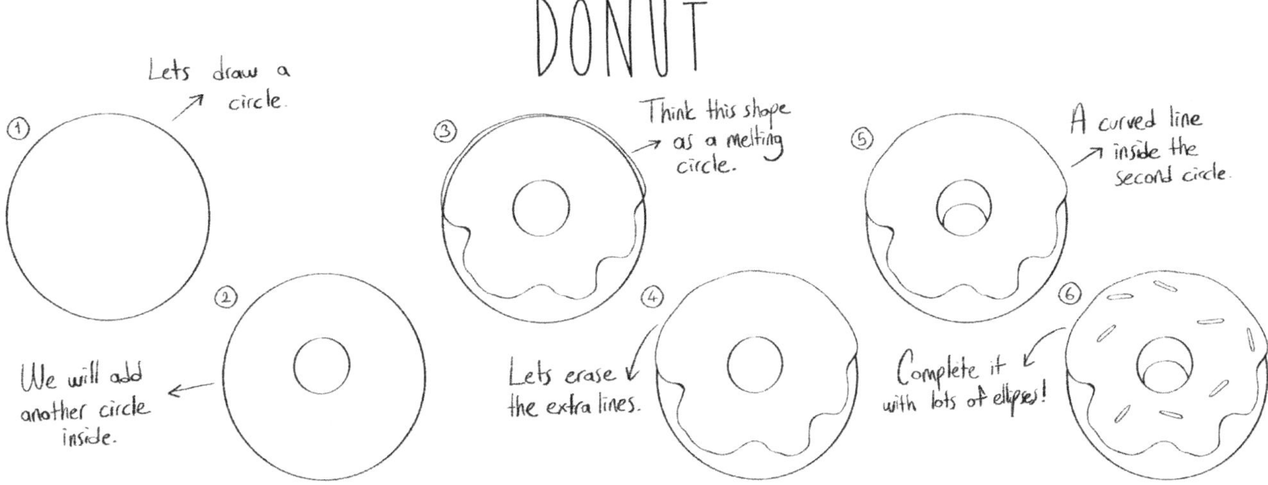
DONUT
1
Lets draw a circle.
2
We will add another circle inside.
3
Think this shape as a melting circle.
4
Lets erase the extra lines.
5
A curved line inside the second circle.
6
Complete it with lots of ellipses!

Your turn to draw some cute food!

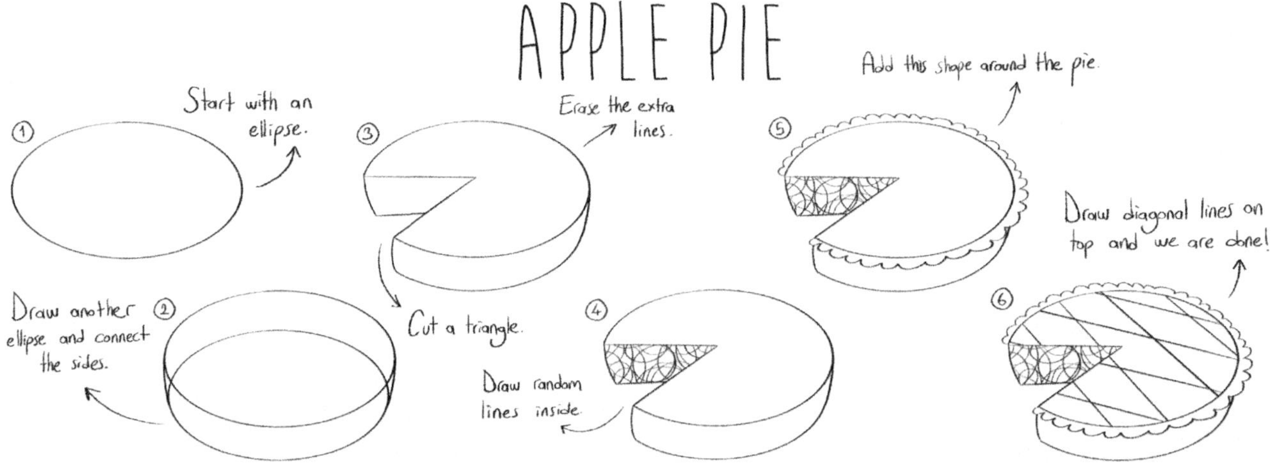
APPLE PIE
1
Start with an ellipse.
Draw another ellipse and connect the sides.
2
3
Erase the extra lines.
Cut a triangle.
4
Draw random lines inside.
Add this shape around the pie.
5
Draw diagonal lines on top and we are done!
6

Your turn to draw some cute food!

GINGERBREAD MAN

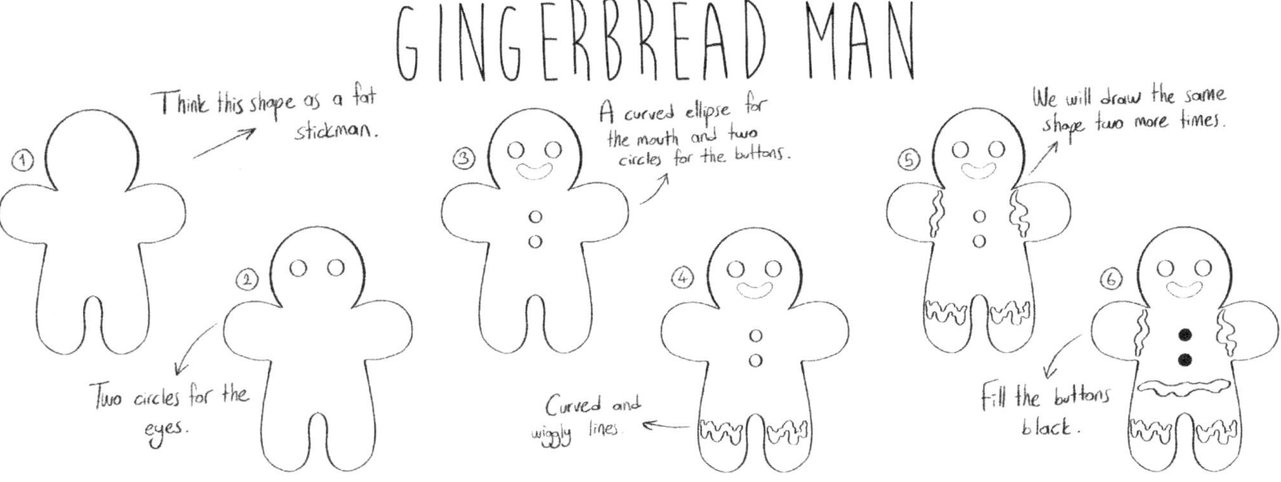
1
Think this shape as a fat stickman.
2
Two circles for the eyes.
3
A curved ellipse for the mouth and two circles for the buttons.
4
Curved and wiggly lines.
5
We will draw the same shape two more times.
6
Fill the buttons black.

Your turn to draw some cute food!

LOLLIPOP

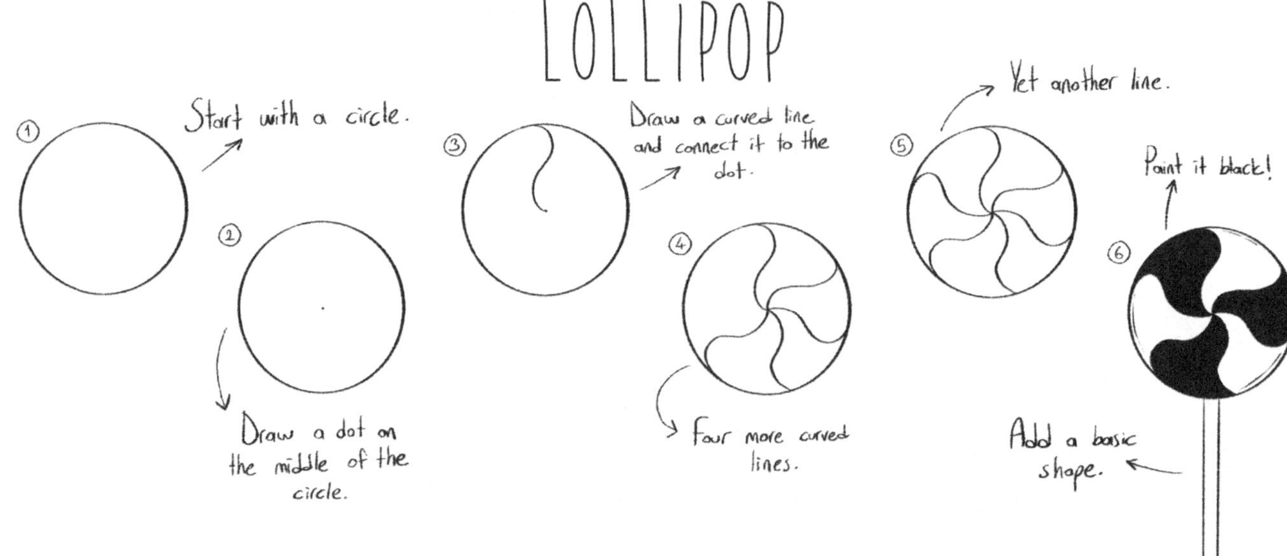

1
Start with a circle.
2
Draw a dot on the middle of the circle.
3
Draw a curved line and connect it to the dot.
4
Four more curved lines.
5
Yet another line.
6
Paint it black!
Add a basic shape.

Your turn to draw some cute food!

CANDY APPLE

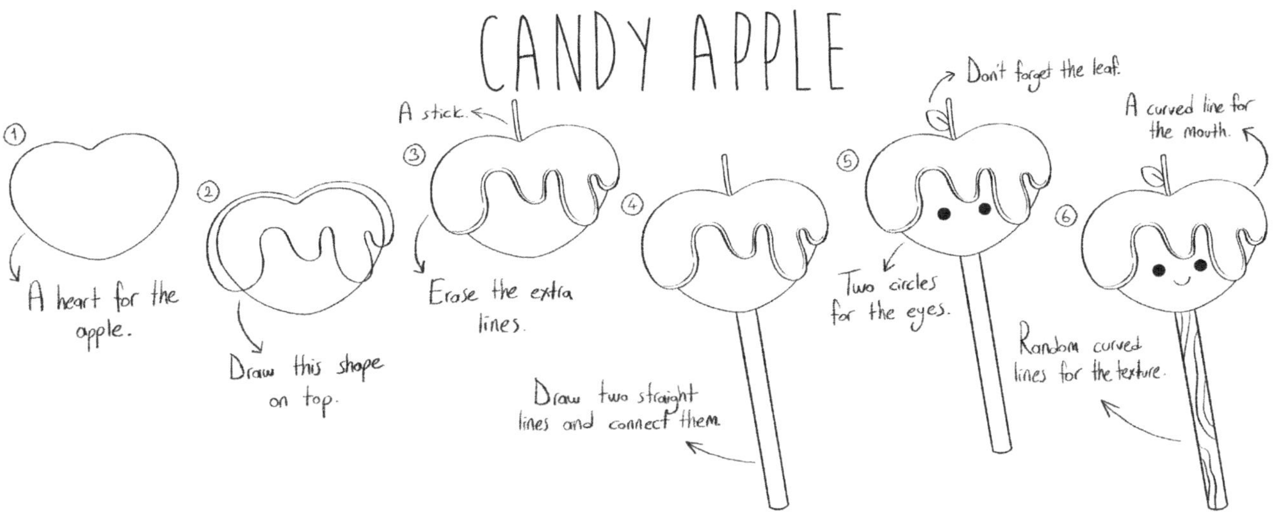

1
A heart for the apple.
2
Draw this shape on top.
A stick.
3
Erase the extra lines.
4
Draw two straight lines and connect them.
Don't forget the leaf.
5
Two circles for the eyes.
A curved line for the mouth.
6
Random curved lines for the texture.

Your turn to draw some cute food!

CANDY CANE
1
Start with a simple line.
2
Draw the same line again on top.
3
Connect those two lines.
4
Draw curved lines inside.
5
Fill them black!
6
Draw a ribbon on top!

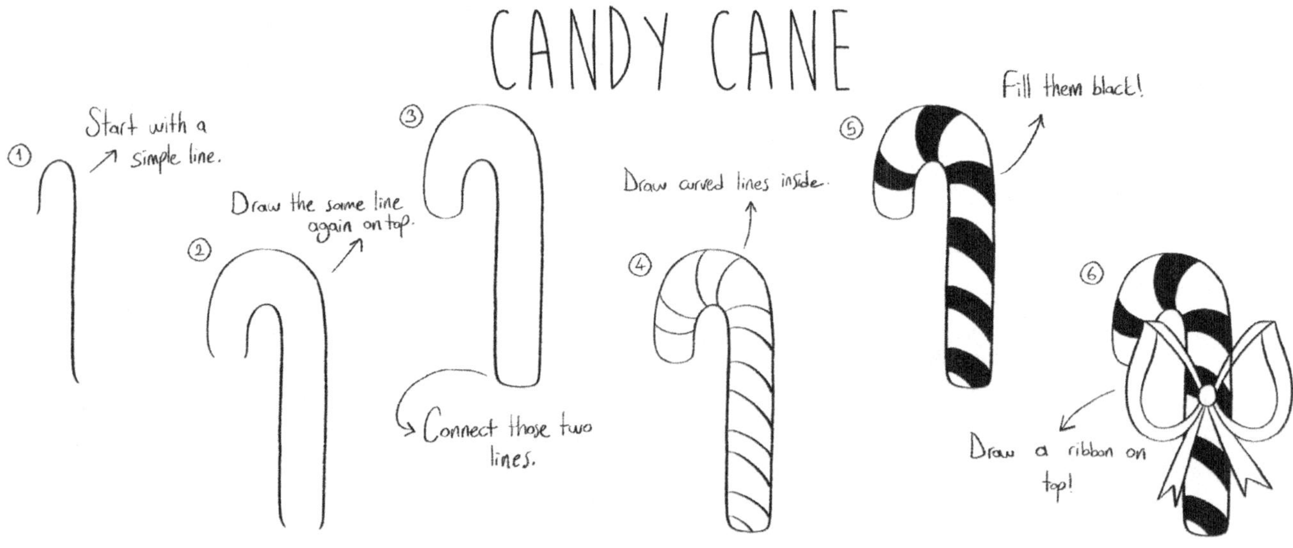

Your turn to draw some cute food!

MARSHMALLOW

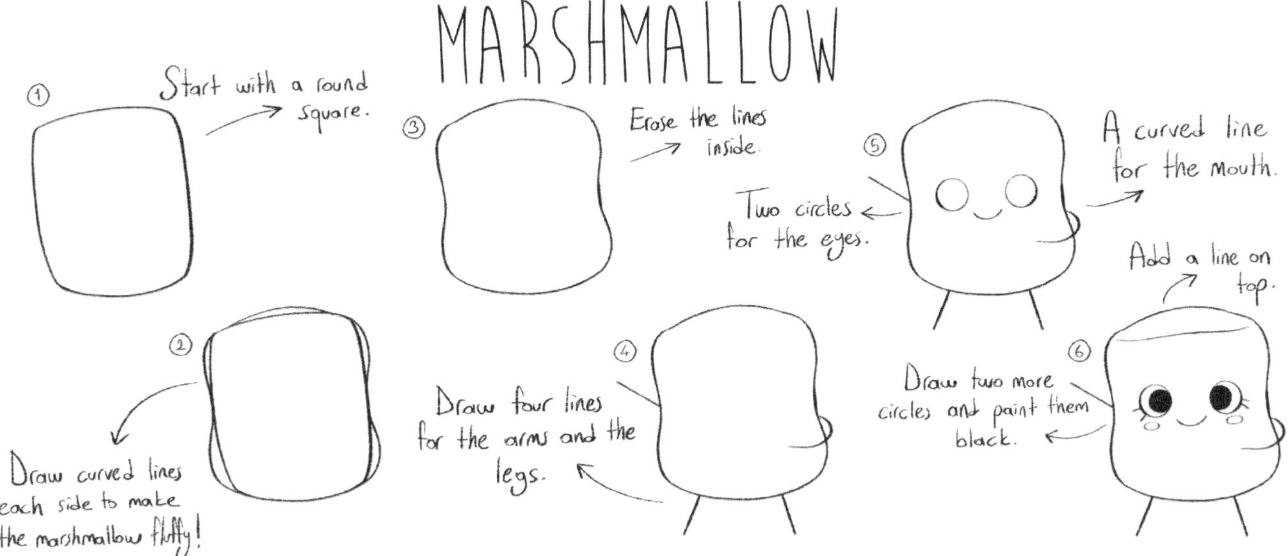

1
Start with a round square.
2
Draw curved lines each side to make the marshmallow fluffy!
3
Erase the lines inside.
4
Draw four lines for the arms and the legs.
5
Two circles for the eyes.
A curved line for the mouth.
6
Add a line on top.
Draw two more circles and paint them black.

Your turn to draw some cute food!

HOT CHOCOLATE

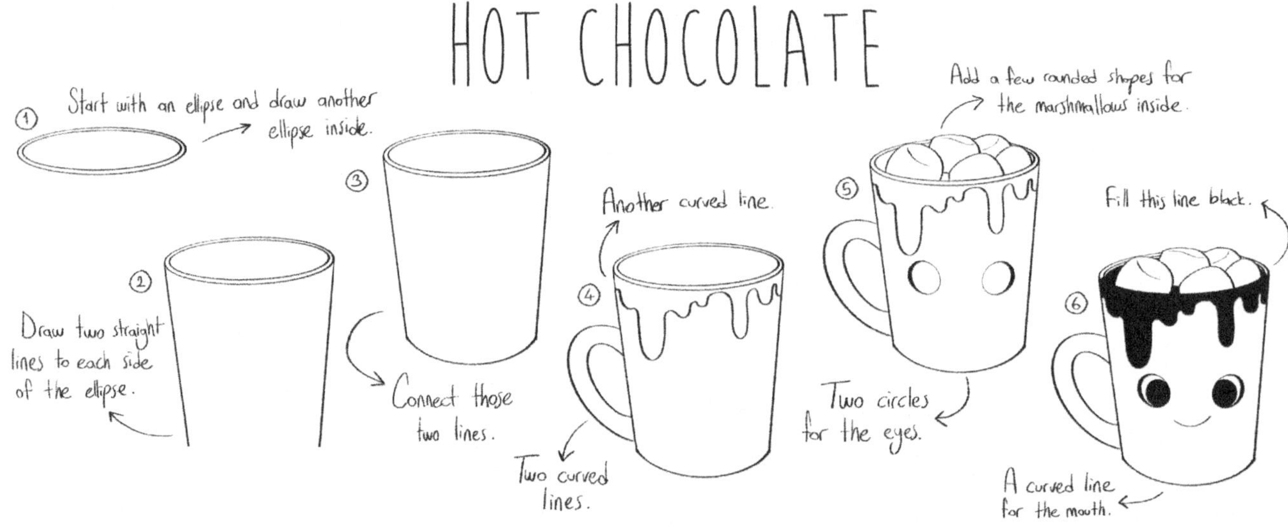
1 Start with an ellipse and draw another ellipse inside.
2 Draw two straight lines to each side of the ellipse.
3 Connect those two lines.
4 Another curved line.
Two curved lines.
5 Add a few rounded shapes for the marshmallows inside.
Two circles for the eyes.
6 Fill this line black.
A curved line for the mouth.

Your turn to draw some cute food!

CANDY

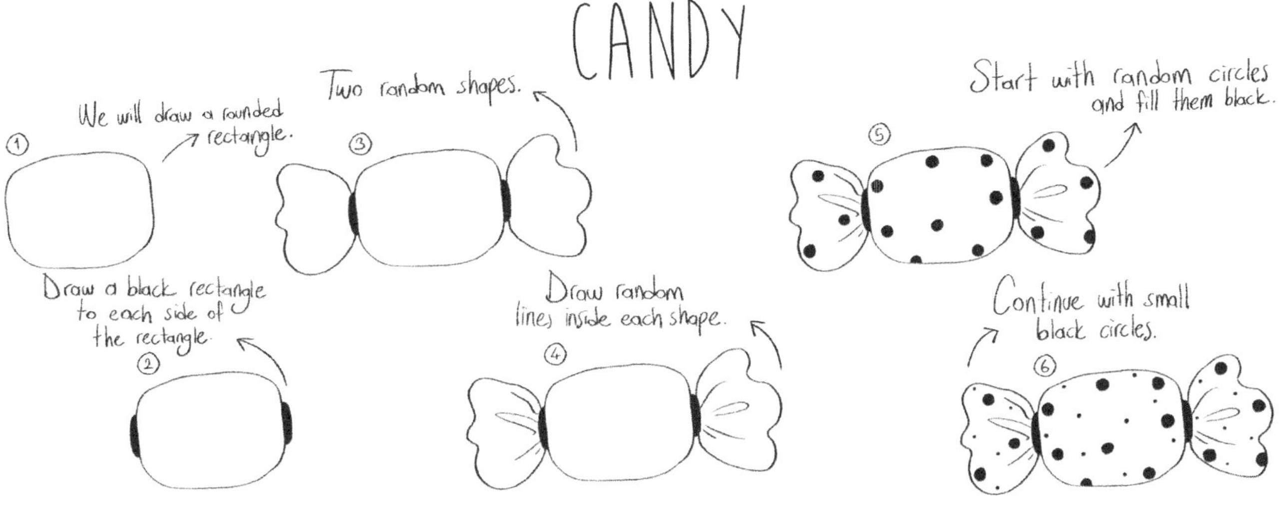

We will draw a rounded rectangle.
Two random shapes.
Start with random circles and fill them black.
Draw a black rectangle to each side of the rectangle.
Draw random lines inside each shape.
Continue with small black circles.

Your turn to draw some cute food!

CHOCOLATE EGG

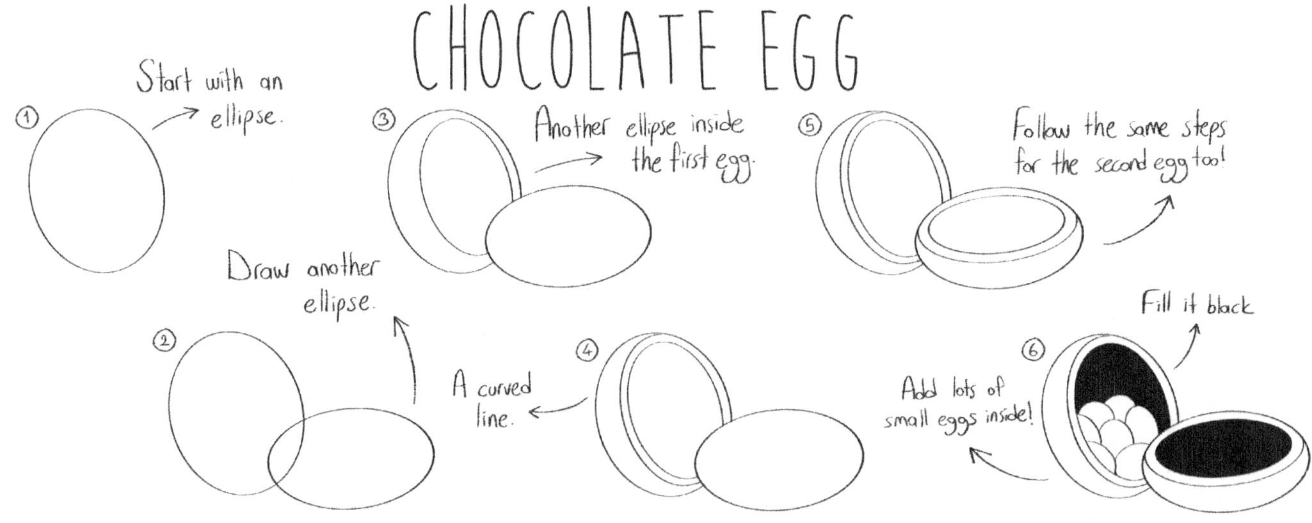

1
Start with an ellipse.
2
Draw another ellipse.
3
Another ellipse inside the first egg.
4
A curved line.
5
Follow the same steps for the second egg too!
6
Fill it black
Add lots of small eggs inside!

Your turn to draw some cute food!

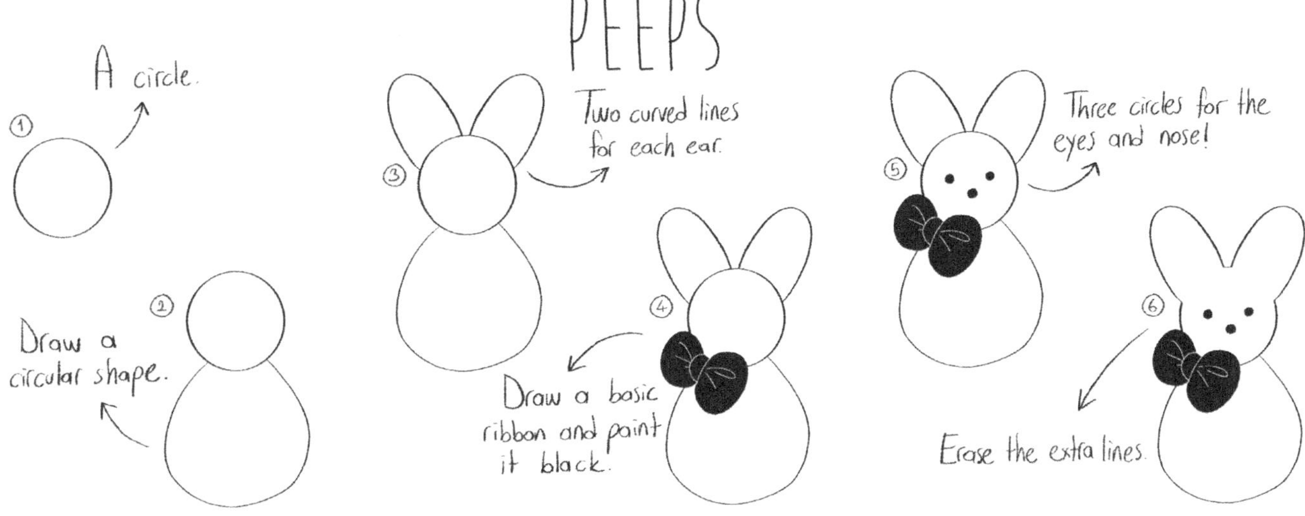
PEEPS
① A circle.
② Draw a circular shape.
③ Two curved lines for each ear.
④ Draw a basic ribbon and paint it black.
⑤ Three circles for the eyes and nose!
⑥ Erase the extra lines.

Your turn to draw some cute food!

CANDY EGGS

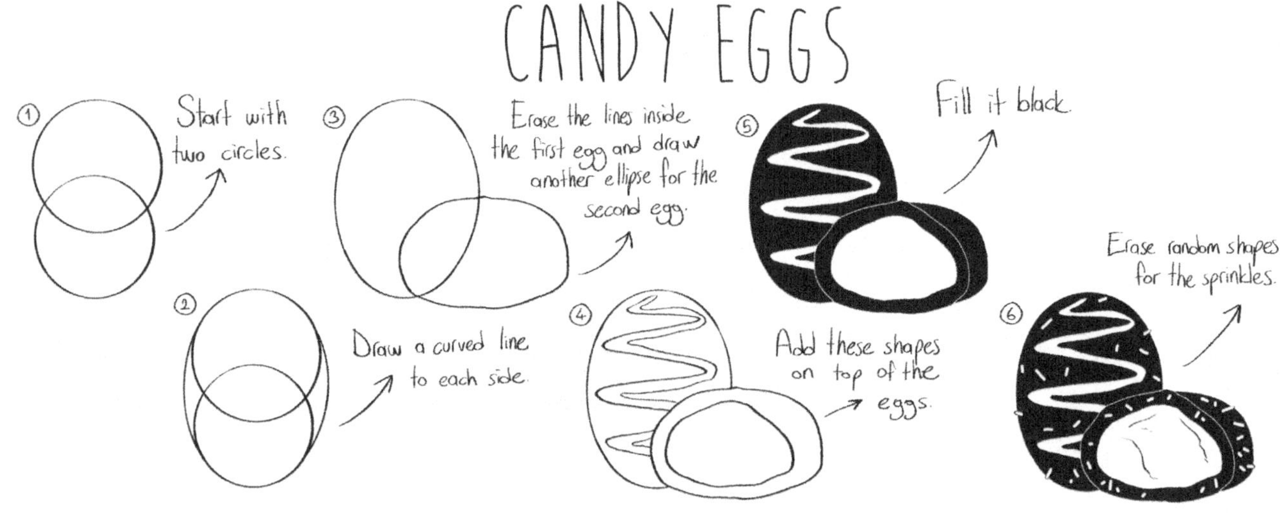

1
Start with two circles.
2
Draw a curved line to each side.
3
Erase the lines inside the first egg and draw another ellipse for the second egg.
4
Add these shapes on top of the eggs.
5
Fill it black.
6
Erase random shapes for the sprinkles.

Your turn to draw some cute food!

JELLY BEANS

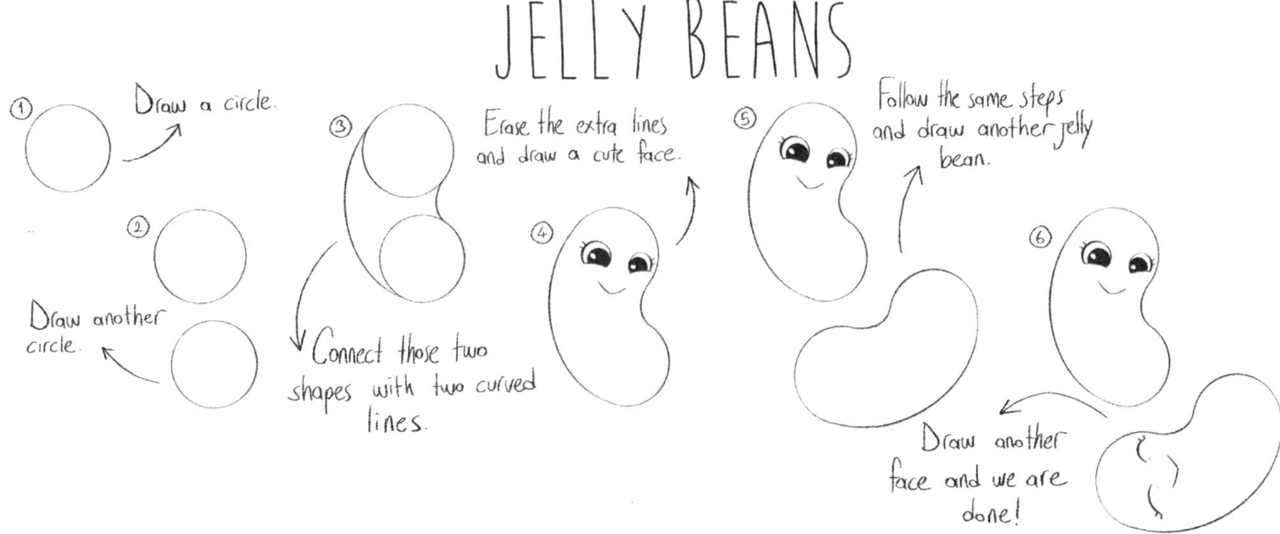

1
Draw a circle.
2
Draw another circle.
3
Connect those two shapes with two curved lines.
4
Erase the extra lines and draw a cute face.
5
Follow the same steps and draw another jelly bean.
6
Draw another face and we are done!

Your turn to draw some cute food!

BOUQUET

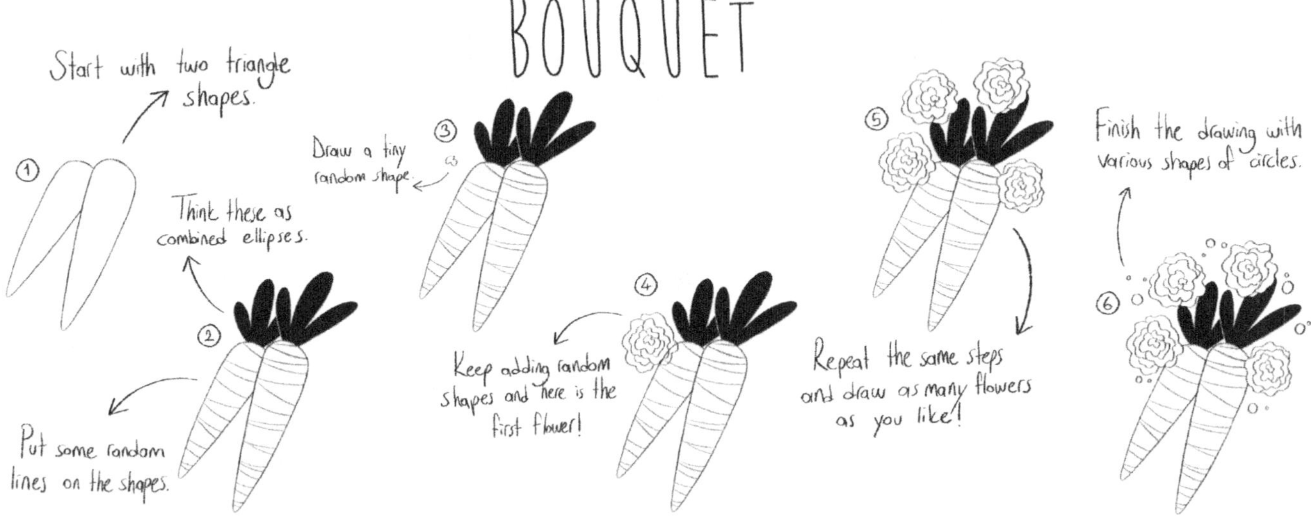

Start with two triangle shapes.
①
Think these as combined ellipses.
②
Put some random lines on the shapes.
Draw a tiny random shape
③
Keep adding random shapes and here is the first flower!
④
⑤
Repeat the same steps and draw as many flowers as you like!
Finish the drawing with various shapes of circles.
⑥

Your turn to draw some cute food!

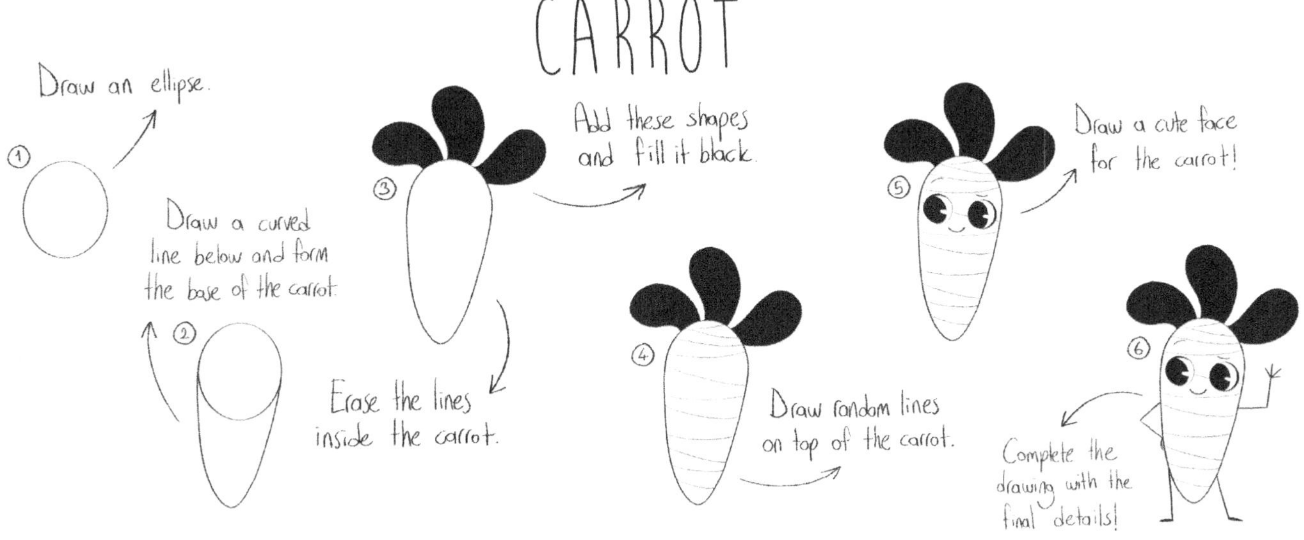
CARROT
1
Draw an ellipse.
2
Draw a curved line below and form the base of the carrot.
3
Add these shapes and fill it black.
Erase the lines inside the carrot.
4
Draw random lines on top of the carrot.
5
Draw a cute face for the carrot!
6
Complete the drawing with the final details!

Your turn to draw some cute food!

CORN

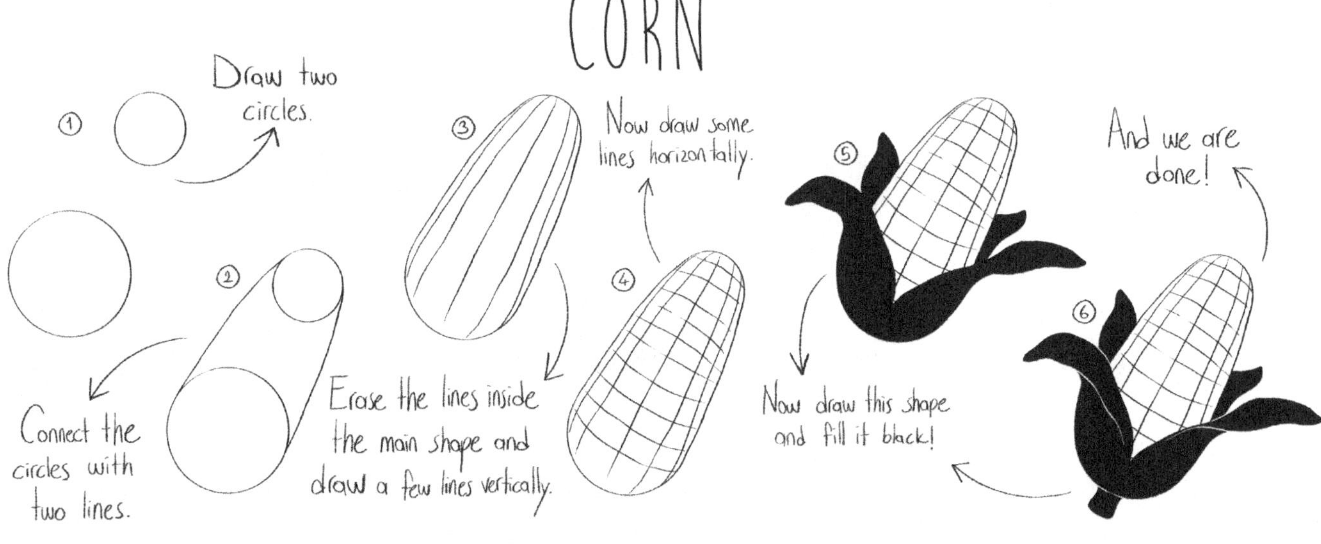

1
Draw two circles.
Connect the circles with two lines.
2
3
Erase the lines inside the main shape and draw a few lines vertically.
4
Now draw some lines horizontally.
5
Now draw this shape and fill it black!
6
And we are done!

Your turn to draw some cute food!

CUPCAKE

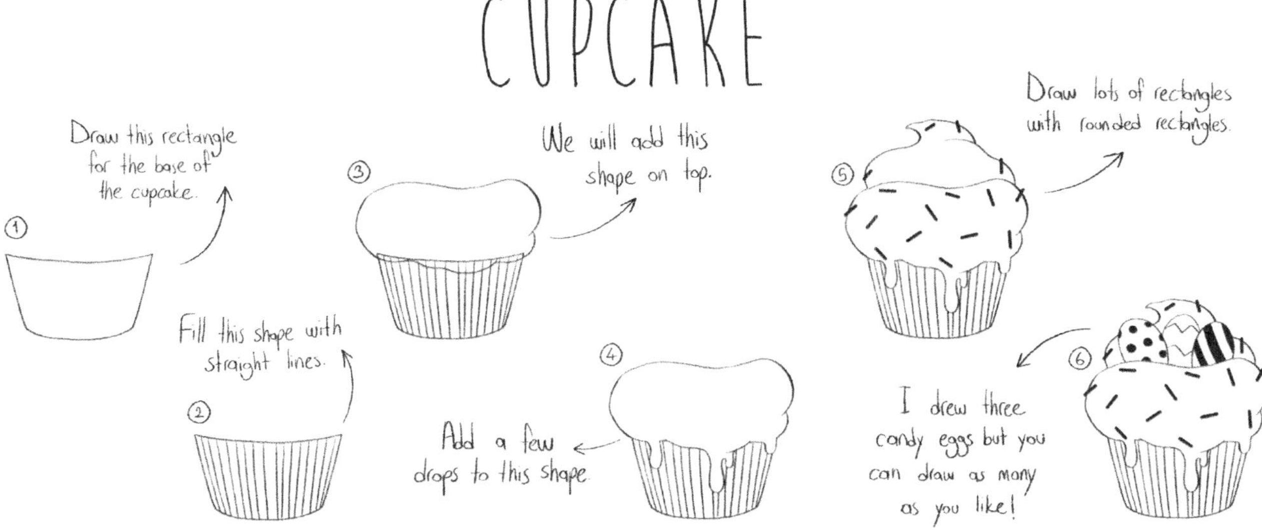

① Draw this rectangle for the base of the cupcake.
② Fill this shape with straight lines.
③ We will add this shape on top.
④ Add a few drops to this shape.
⑤ Draw lots of rectangles with rounded rectangles.
⑥ I drew three candy eggs but you can draw as many as you like!

Your turn to draw some cute food!

BAGELS
1
Start with a circular shape.
2
Draw a circle here.
3
Lets draw another circular shape.
4
Draw a line to the second shape.
5
Lets draw another circle here.
6
Add lots of short lines on top.

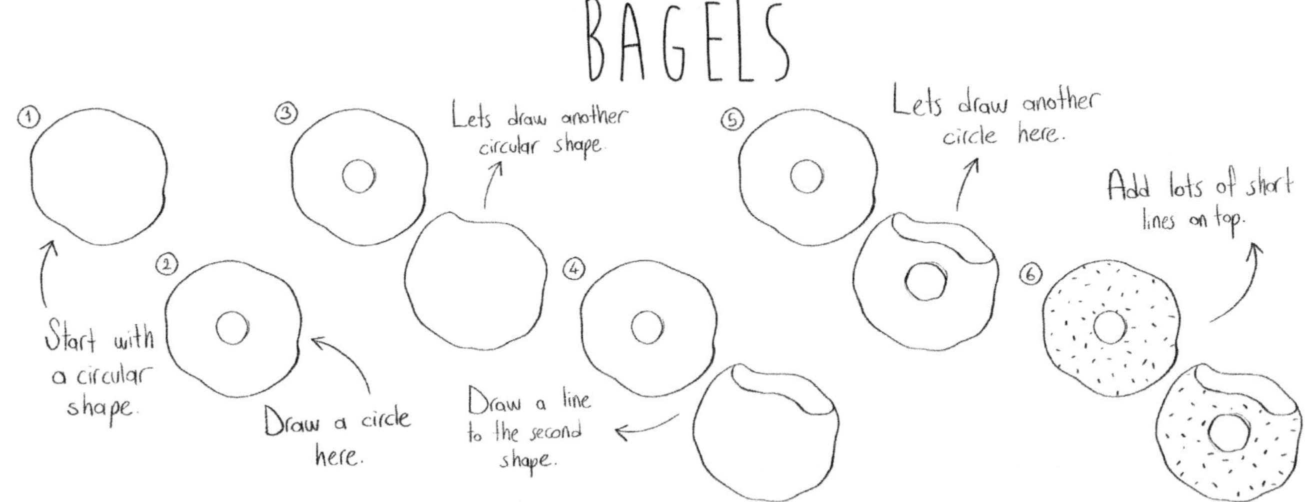

Your turn to draw some cute food!

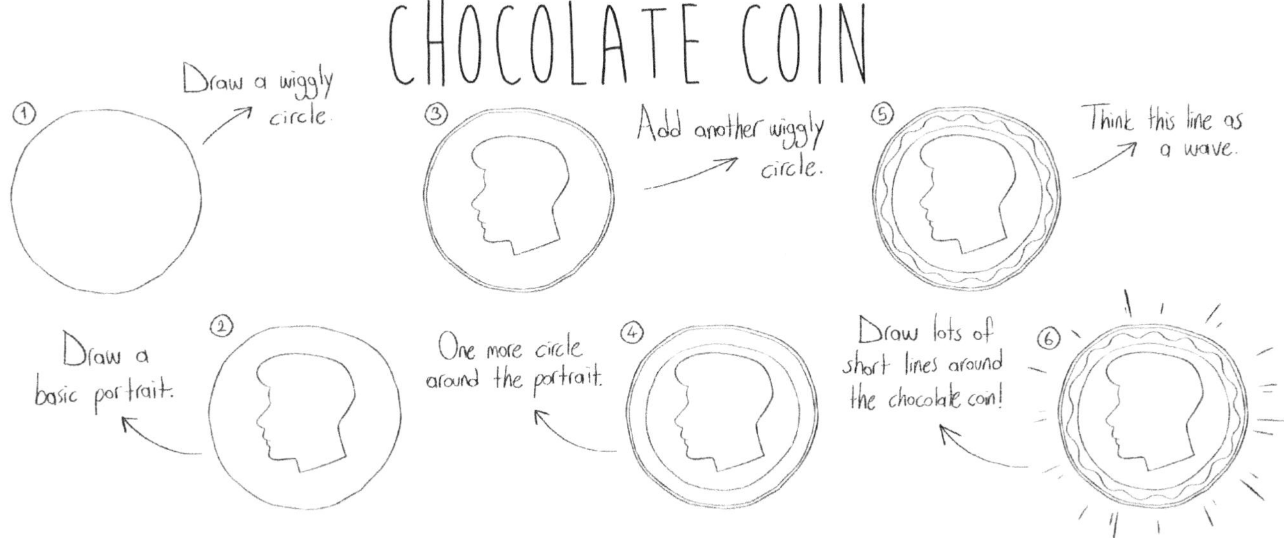
CHOCOLATE COIN
1
Draw a wiggly circle.
2
Draw a basic portrait.
3
Add another wiggly circle.
4
One more circle around the portrait.
5
Think this line as a wave.
6
Draw lots of short lines around the chocolate coin!

Your turn to draw some cute food!

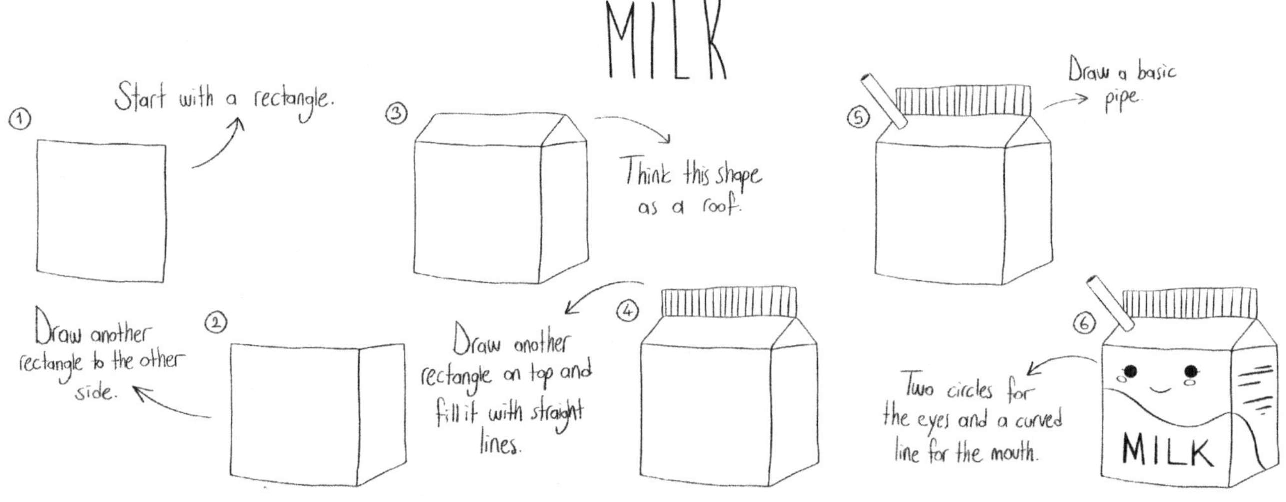
MILK
1
Start with a rectangle.
2
Draw another rectangle to the other side.
3
Think this shape as a roof.
4
Draw another rectangle on top and fill it with straight lines.
5
Draw a basic pipe.
6
Two circles for the eyes and a curved line for the mouth.
MILK

Your turn to draw some cute food!

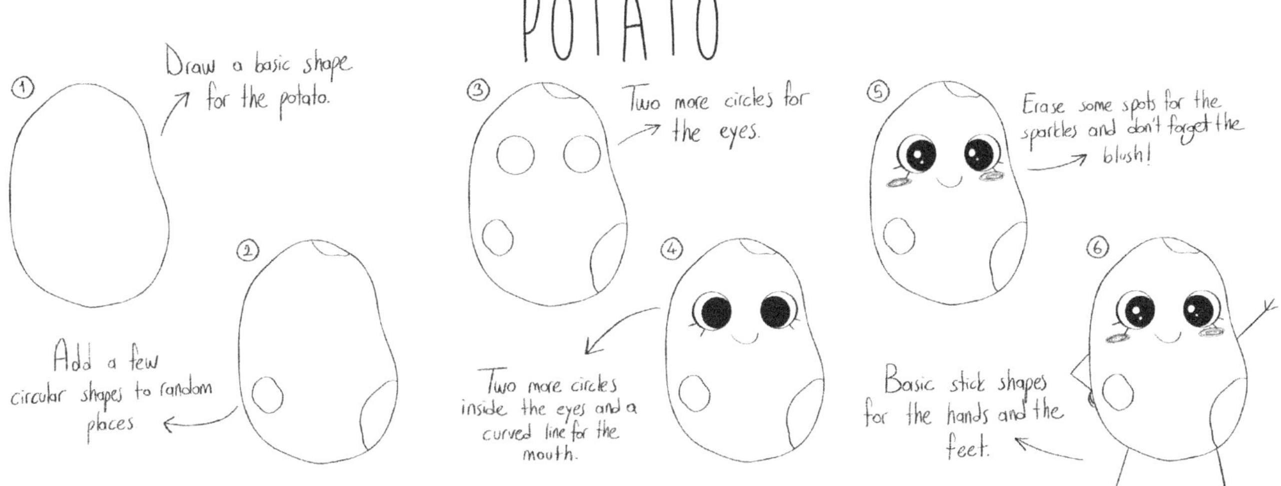
POTATO
1
Draw a basic shape for the potato.
2
Add a few circular shapes to random places
3
Two more circles for the eyes.
4
Two more circles inside the eyes and a curved line for the mouth.
5
Erase some spots for the sparkles and don't forget the blush!
6
Basic stick shapes for the hands and the feet.

Your turn to draw some cute food!

CABBAGE

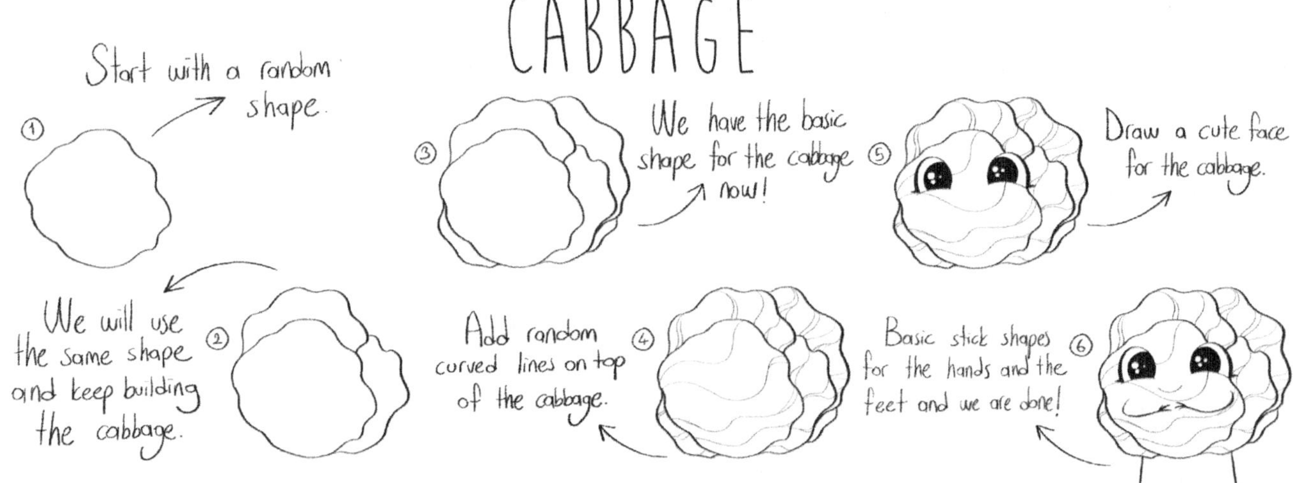
Start with a random shape.
① ② ③ ④ ⑤ ⑥
We will use the same shape and keep building the cabbage.
We have the basic shape for the cabbage now!
Add random curved lines on top of the cabbage.
Draw a cute face for the cabbage.
Basic stick shapes for the hands and the feet and we are done!

Your turn to draw some cute food!

PIE

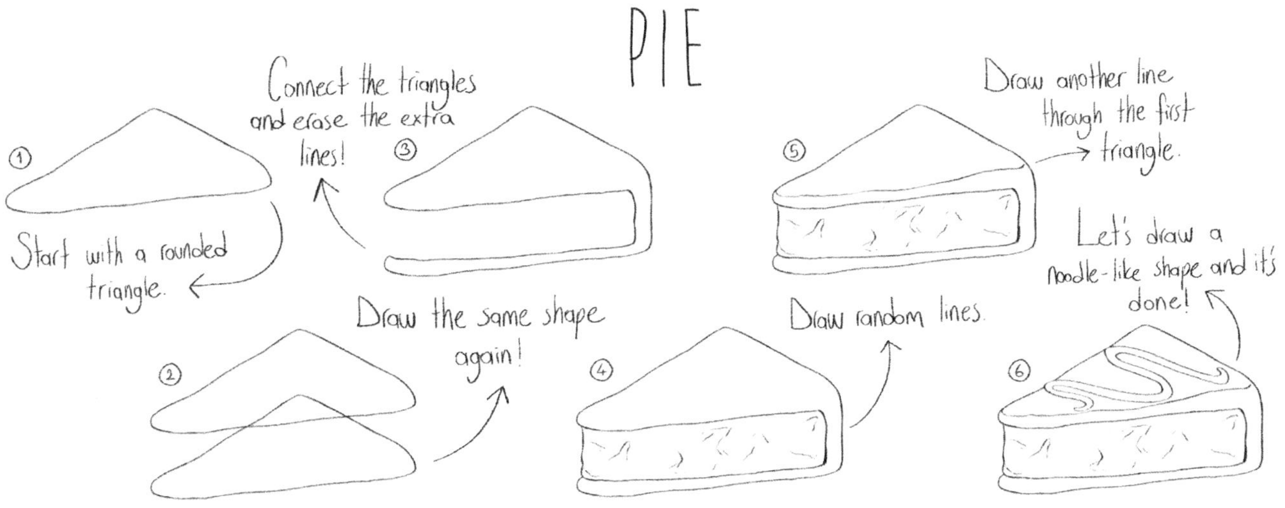

Connect the triangles and erase the extra lines!
Draw another line through the first triangle.
Start with a rounded triangle.
Let's draw a noodle-like shape and it's done!
Draw the same shape again!
Draw random lines.

Your turn to draw some cute food!

CANDY CORN

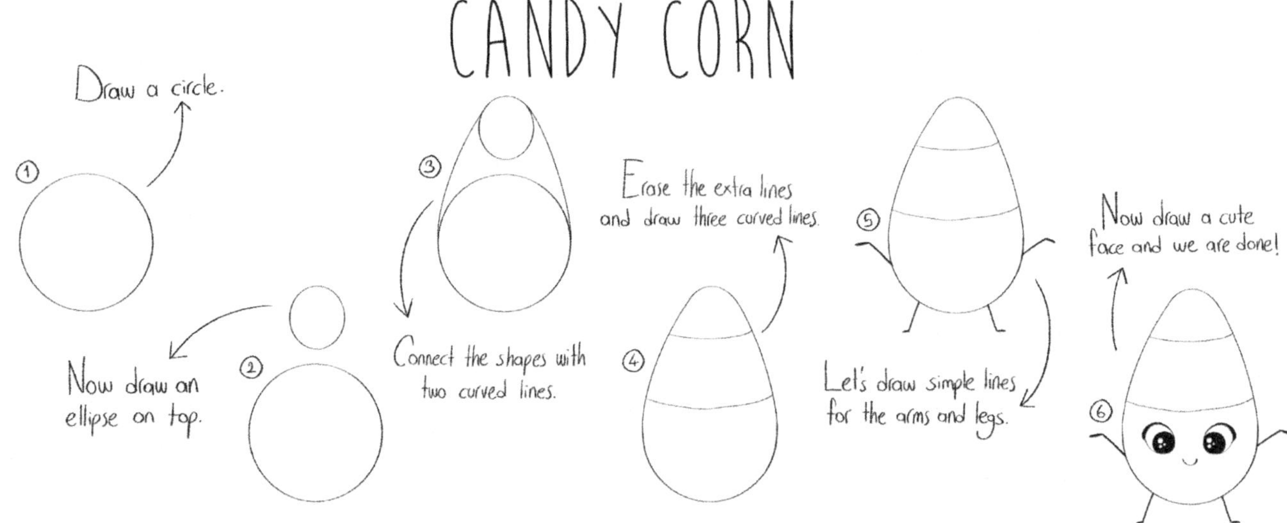

1
Draw a circle.
2
Now draw an ellipse on top.
3
Connect the shapes with two curved lines.
4
Erase the extra lines and draw three curved lines.
5
Let's draw simple lines for the arms and legs.
6
Now draw a cute face and we are done!

Your turn to draw some cute food!

COFFEE
1
Start with an ellipse.
3
Fill these area black.
5
Let's add this shape.
2
Draw a curved line inside the ellipse.
Now draw this shape for the cup.
4
Now draw a few curved shapes here. We are done!
6

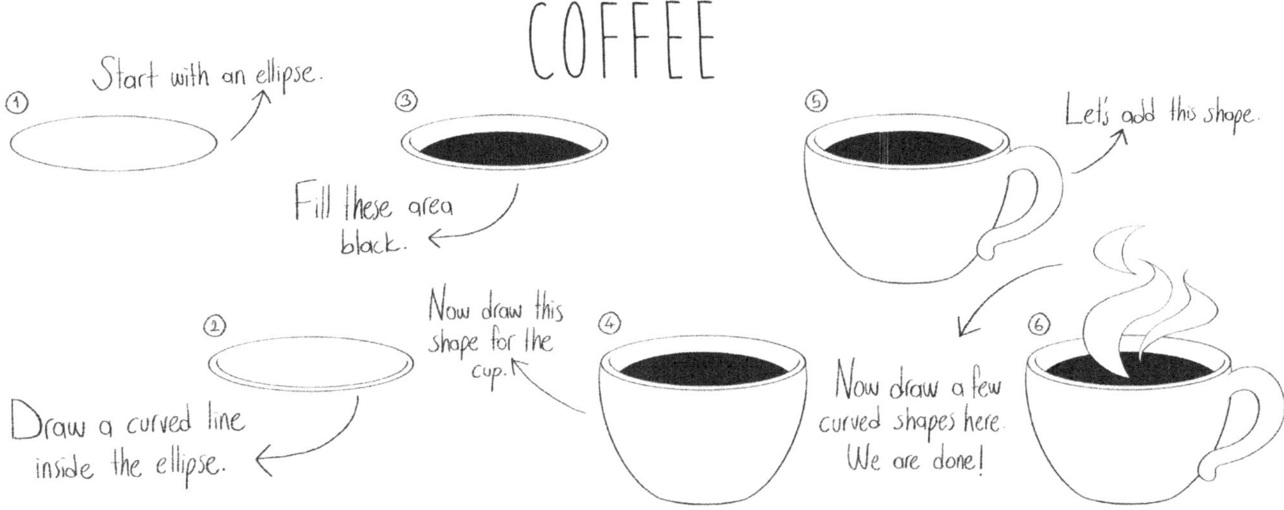

Your turn to draw some cute food!

Made in the USA
Monee, IL
29 November 2022

18820515R00024